TO HARRY N IDA

BRIDGEMAN

De Grazia

1981

The World of De Grazia

The World of

An Artist of the American Southwest

By Harry Redl

With a Text by Buck Saunders
Foreword by Gary Avey

CHRYSALIS PUBLISHING, LTD.
PHOENIX, ARIZONA

Acknowledgements:

The author owes a debt of gratitude to a great number of people who have helped with this book in various ways.

Susan, Elizabeth, Bill and "Two-Guns" of the Gallery in the Sun staff have made the many hours of work there a pleasure with their unfailing friendliness.

Cassandra Hotchkiss and Tish Holland have helped immeasurably and selflessly. So has Richard Smith with advice and encouragement. Bob Mullen was never too busy to discuss the project and contribute valuable ideas. John Morton went out of his way to smooth out production problems. Many thanks to all these fine people.

Garrison Cattell adopted this book from its very start and has worked tirelessly to see it through to completion. He steadfastly refused to allow any compromise on quality or deadlines, was available at night and on weekends with unflagging enthusiasm and fought many a battle on behalf of the book. It is almost impossible to adequately thank this extraordinary man for his decency and friendship.

Last but by no means least, the author wishes to acknowledge the contributions made by Buck Saunders and his wife Leobarda. Without their help, their experience and their awesome patience, this book may not have been possible. With great generosity, they shared their knowledge, answered a thousand questions, checked every fact in the book, furnished material and listened kindly to tales of woe. Buck Saunders wrote Part Four of this book and no one could ask for a more understanding writer nor a more reliable one. Not only have they infused the project with dignity, but in the process they have enriched the authors life.

First Edition
Library of Congress Catalog Card Number 81-67693
Composed and printed in the United States of America.

CONTENTS:

FOREWORD:
By Gary Avey

The fusion of the man and his land pours forth — the force of pure colors pulsating upon white canvas . . . the art and the artist become a phenomenon in the American southwest. Such has been the case with the vivid, sensitive, simple works of Ettore "Ted" De Grazia.

But how did this come about?

Where did Ted first uncover his artistic sense of awareness?

I would like to suggest a scene from a time much earlier in this century: The afternoon rain departed, leaving the normally dusty slag heap from the copper mine glistening like a freshly fallen rainbow. The little mining town of Morenci, hideden away in southeastern Arizona, rang with the laughter and shouts of children suddlenly released from weather-imposed household bondage. Among the throng, young Ted paused — his eyes scanning piles of rain-washed rocks. The normally tawny colors now also included cadmium red and zinc white. And throughout this stony spectrum were bits and pieces of Ted's favorite treasure, shiny, naturally faceted nuggets of iron pyrite — "fool's gold".

Ted was surrounded by colorful beauty which was overlooked by other children. Had his father, an Italian hard rock miner, not immigrated to America, Ted's youthful visions might have included the artistic triumphs that abound in Florence, or Rome. But instead of Ghiberti's "Gates of Paradise", Ted's eyes beheld the vibrant colors of rough stones which later formed the earth-solid base for his artistic expression.

To follow were several years in Italy before returning to Morenci to finish high school, two B.A. degrees from the University of Arizona — one in music and one in art — work in Mexico City with the great Diego Rivera and José Clemente Orozco, and a Masters Degree, again from the University of Arizona, with his thesis on the relation of color to sound.

Early in his career Ted had some successful showings in Mexico, and some abysmal failures in Arizona. But as his style evolved from powerful revolutionary statements, into Plangraphic shapes, into simple forms, color emerged as the dominant theme with pure chromatic effects.

About this time Raymond Carlson, then editor (and philosophical

---

Mr. Avey is Editor of Arizona Highways Magazine.

architect) of the emerging *Arizona Highways Magazine,* became acquainted with Ted, and his work first appeared on the magazine's pages in 1941. In a 1949 article regarding De Grazia's work, Carlson wrote, "They have honesty and strength, reflecting the singularity of purpose and the integrity of a painter who has remained true to his beliefs in the face of adverse criticism and begrudging recognition." As Ted's art appeared in the magazine, people throughout Arizona, America, and eventually the world, began to respond to the frank, yet sensitive emotions he displayed on canvas.

My own first exposure to the man and the art of Ted De Grazia in the late forties, mirrored somewhat his usual controversial position in artistic circles. Although only nine years old, I was well-accustomed to listening to the conversations of my art editor father, George Avey, and his artist and photographer friends. On one occasion I could sense his restrained displeasure as Raymond Carlson described the upcoming magazine devoted in large measure to his bearded friend sitting there with us. The more lavish Raymond's praise of Ted's art became, the more I could feel my father's structured architectural education, building professional resistance to this free-flowing painter from southern Arizona. Raymond's will prevailed, much to the joy of hundreds of thousands of readers over the years, and even George had to admit that Ted had a way of communicating his feelings in an exciting and successful way.

Ted's following grew, and with their enthusiastic response came a newfound sense of surety for the artist. With extensive reproductions of his work in the marketplaces, ranging from elegant serigraphs to tiny wind chimes, rumbles began to emerge from critics and others in the artistic community. But the dedication and love from his fans balanced out such comments as, "over commercialized", "sold out", and others not befitting the printed word.

In truth, of course, it's our own experiential data and peer perceptions that shape today's taste in art, and time will determine those creations that are to endure. But given the tens of thousands of dedicated De Grazia followers, it is not difficult to defend the statement that he is ". . . a legend in his own time".

Is the art of Ettore "Ted" De Grazia representative of his honest feelings, or, as some critics have remarked, contrived evolvement for increasing sales to the public? Well, during a pleasant mid-day luncheon some years ago, I remarked to Ted about the beautiful bracelet he was wearing. A massive hammered bronze band embellished with a single glittering golden nugget. When Ted explained the bracelet, he summed up my own perception of my lifetime friend. The nugget you see, was "fool's gold", while the thick innocent band was in fact solid gold.

He has touched the land . . . he learned the secret . . . he has shared it with the people.

Part One

THE MAN

By Harry Redl

10

11

In a rambling adobe building on the outskirts of Tucson, Arizona, the telephone rings. The room around the desk looks like a Sheriff's office in an old Western film. There is even an iron-barred gate, as if to a jail-cell, leading to a storage room, with bunches of keys hanging from it.

The man who answers the call could well play the Sheriff in that same picture, with his scuffed Cowboy boots and his weathered Western hat, his grizzled beard and a pinch of snuff tucked under the inside of his lower lip.

"Sorry, Ma'am, but we close at 4:00 p.m. every day," he says to the caller, than listens for a moment and continues, "Me? Oh, I'm the caretaker," and hangs up.

Well, yes and no.

The man in the well-worn ranchhand clothes is none other than Ettore "Ted" De Grazia, the most reproduced artist in the world. An estimated 100 million of his images have gone out into the world and have touched the hearts of his legion of admirers. He is the essence of the American Southwest, a legend in his own time, a natural phenomenon. A most sophisticated primitive, a gentle iconoclast, a visionary man of action. And no, he does not do floors anymore.

On the other hand, he is a caretaker of sorts. The Gallery in the Sun is his dream, realized in desert materials from the countryside around it. He built it himself, with the help of some friends. And he takes good care of them. Like his paintings, they are his children, his ninos. He is the nucleus of that world and in that sense, he is indeed the caretaker.

As behooves a legend, De Grazia is surrounded by myth and speculation. Since he hates to talk about himself, it is often difficult to verify the very simplest facts of his life, let alone some of the wild stories that circulate about him. Indeed, De Grazia encourages the spreading of the lore, by rarely denying a rumor, no matter how bizarre; by his reluctance to discuss that portion of his life which he considers private and inviolate. De Grazia not only closes shop at 4:00 p.m. every afternoon, but also literally vanishes. Only a few close friends ever see him after that.

12

Some time ago, two business associates of his drove all the way down from Phoenix to hand over $67,000 in royalties to De Grazia. Some mechanical troubles along the way delayed the party and the car swerved into the driveway of the gallery a few minutes after 4:00, just as the painter was locking up the gates. "Well, I told you we close at 4:00," De Grazia said softly. "So, see you tomorrow morning at 10:00!" There was nothing else for the businessmen to do, but spend the night in a motel and hand over the check the next morning.

Recently, De Grazia told a visitor, "More and more I want less and less. You know, the most precious thing in my life at this stage is privacy. It is not that I am against people. After all, it is people who have made me what I am today."

13

For these reasons, very little is known about his private life. He is open to scrutiny from 10:00 a.m. to 4:00 p.m. only, and not too many truly important things happen to a man between these hours.

During the gallery hours, however, he gives of himself unstintingly. It is then that he takes care of that part of his world that belongs to the public. He talks to visitors, signs prints and cards for the people from California, Illinois and Maine and points between, who daily flock to the Gallery in the Sun in Tucson. From all walks of life, they come with a touching reverence, a disarming awe. De Grazia's patience with them is at times heroic.

"Listen, these are my people. Without them, where would I be? How can I not love them and accommodate them?" He signs a print here, a greeting card there, a book. Then an elderly woman from Delaware comes up to him with a small enamel piece and says, "Mr. De Grazia, this is for my husband at home. I realize it is too small for you to sign, but could you just touch it for him?" And De Grazia does so, chats with her for a while, pecks her on the cheek.

What sort of man is this? What makes him so private and so public at the same time? What is at the heart of all the contradictions that make up De Grazia? Reviled by his detractors, beloved by his friends from brain surgeons to illiterate braceros, De Grazia moves through his world like a man who has found his center of gravity. The man who once said, "My work belongs to the public art world, for all to see. I remain a private individual" is a biograghers nightmare.

There is, of course, his work and as reticent as De Grazia is about his private life, as lavish is he with his images. Those, who are able to read between his brushstrokes will smile knowingly, for it is all there. The pain, the joy, the preoccupations and the dreams. At the confluence of all these forces must be De Grazia, the man. And there are some hard facts as well as some biographical data to guide us along. Perhaps that is a good point to start our quest.

Ettore De Grazia was born on June 14, 1909 in Morenci, a mining town in what was then the Territory of Arizona, as the proud descendant of three generations of Italian hard-rock miners. "You cannot start out lower than that, in every sense of the word," he would remark later.

De Grazia's father worked in the large copper mines Phelps Dodge operated in the area. In fact, the ore was the sole reason for the existence of Morenci. All the Mexicans, Indians and other assorted nationalities were there only for the copper, and like any other company town, Morenci had few traditions other than sweat and ore.

It is difficult to imagine, that one of the rough-and-tumble mining camps of the frontier days, with such blatantly commercial motivations, could produce a sensitivity and irrepressible creative force such as Ted De Grazia. Unless one remembers the free-form graffiti of an open-pit coppermine: the joyous turquoise of the veins of copper ore, the darkbrown stains of iron deposits, the sharp yellows of the sand, the surrounding burnt-sienna landscapes and, after the rare rainfalls, the wisps of green, the desert flowers of a wet spring.

Ettore roamed those wild hills and mountains endlessly as a young boy, undoubtedly absorbing the desert colors and their wild configurations. These first impressions must have left indelible marks on the boy, which would ultimately turn him into the kind of painter he would become: a celebrant of the American Southwest.

In 1920, when Ettore turned eleven, his family packed up and moved back to Italy, where De Grazia spent the next five years. When the family finally returned to Morenci in 1925, Ettore had forgotten most of his English. He entered first grade at the age of 16 and one of his teachers decided to Anglicize the exotic "Ettore" into "Theodore", because it was easier to spell. Ultimately "Theodore" became "Ted" and has remained so ever since. When young Ted graduated at the age of 23, he was a full-fledged American.

During these years Ted De Grazia had developed a deep interest in music and the arts, between stints of working in the mines alongside his father.

In 1932 De Grazia left for Tucson to study music at the University of Arizona. Money was scarce in those days and De Grazia paid for his education with a variety of odd jobs. One of the more colorful of these occupations was playing the trumpet in local bands and houses of ill repute. De Grazia describes his style on the horn as "loud and lousy", but made as much as $1 per night.

15

Shortly before earning a Bachelors degree, De Grazia abandoned his studies for the time being, in search of a career and matrimony. It soon became clear, however, that he was not yet ready to settle down for good. There were all all these curiosities to be satisfied, all those creative urges to be dealt with and he drifted away from commerce, out of his marriage and deeper and deeper into his art.

He started to paint furiously and experimented in all forms of expression, particularly ceramics, which was to become a lifelong interest. Along the way, he developed a unique turquoise glaze based on copper ore rather than the iron-based glazes that were in general use.

In between De Grazia went on extensive trips through the land he loved so much, Arizona and Mexico. Since most of the Mexicans he had known in Morenci came from Sonora and Chihuahua, he was particularly drawn toward those provinces and came to know them intimately. Being fluent in Spanish, he had no trouble at all blending into the land, becoming a part of it.

In 1941, these peregrinations resulted in a show of paintings entitled: "Dust of Mexico". Although the public, not to mention the critics, paid little attention to the efforts of this newcomer, he did impress some knowledgable viewers. The reputable magazine "Arizona Highways" reviewed his showing enthusiastically.

The respected editor of the periodical, Raymond Carlson, wrote, ". . . you should spend some time following the vagrant country roads that ramble about northern Sonora and learn to know and understand the people you meet along those roads. Then you will like the paintings of De Grazia."

To the question put by a visitor, what made De Grazia become an artist, he recently answered, "Mainly that I wanted to get out of the mines. But I never thought I would make money painting. I suppose I painted because I wanted to paint. However, sometimes I don't even know if I like painting. Or maybe I do it because I hate it."

Hate it or love it, he produced a huge body of work in those days and for a long time it seemed that he would be proven right. Namely, that he would not be able to make money with his art.

Not satisfied with his progress, De Grazia decided to go to Mexico City in 1942, to further his studies of painting. What made him choose Mexico City, aside from his deep love for that culture, De Grazia explains like this: "If you want to learn to paint, you better spend some time with great painters. Since El Greco and Gaugin were dead, I had to go to Mexico City to see Diego Rivera and José Orozco."

These two immortal Mexican artists were engaged in their mural work around Mexico City and they received the "Norteamericano" most graciously. De Grazia felt that he was treated as a fellow artist, rather than as a novice. He worked with them, often performing menial tasks such as cleaning brushes, mixing paint, moving scaffolding and sweeping floors. It was no vacation, living on as little as 10¢ a day, sleeping in the park at night with the Indians who had drifted into the big city. But for the young artist it was exhilarating, a heady experience and De Grazia made the most of it, always observing, always absorbing.

It proved to be a very fruitful time indeed and De Grazia was present while Rivera painted at the second floor of the Palacio Nationale. Orozco was then completing his celebrated murals at the Hospital of Jesus Nazarene in Mexico City. Cortés himself is said to have founded the hospital and the bones of the Conquistador were found there. De Grazia worked with Orozco and aside from the artistic satisfaction must have savored the historic ground he was

18

treading. This was his world. About his two mentors De Grazia has said, "They were not the easiest people in the world to work for, but they knew their art and I learned quickly."

In the end, Rivera and Orozco sponsored an exhibition of De Grazia's paintings at Mexico City's prestigious Palacio de Bellas Artes in November 1942. It was a great success. Mexico's most respected magazine "Hoy" reviewed the show in glowing terms and it gave De Grazia's spirits a considerable lift then and in the hard times still to come. The program of the show announced him as a "pintor norteamericano primitivo", although it could be argued that what was perceived as primitive was really a directness of feeling, a groping for honesty.

His two illustrious sponsors felt that there was a budding talent here that would ultimately develop into true significance. Diego Rivera wrote, for instance: "His paintings interest me profoundly not only because of his brilliant artistic gift. His personal feeling is of such originality, that it overcomes much of his influences by virtue of some intangible force, perhaps the subconscious. When fully developed as a painter, De Grazia is sure to become a prominent figure in American art."

José Clemente Orozco concurred with this prophecy, "His work has all the simplicity, freshness and power of youth . . . He will be one of the best American painters some day."

De Grazia returned to Arizona in 1943, confidently offering the Mexico City show to his Alma Mater, the University of Arizona in Tucson. To his dismay, the show that was such a success abroad, was turned down in his own backyard.

Many years later, when De Grazia was already established and sought after, that same University approached him to hang a retrospective exhibition of 100 of his paintings. Remembering the earlier snub with some bitterness, De Grazia replied, "I needed you in 1943. Where were you then? Now, I don't need you any more." Whereupon the University answered, "But now we need you!"

De Grazia relented and the retrospective show was exhibited with such an echo, that the University asked the artist to donate these paintings to the permanent collection of their art department. "I didn't want the paintings to wind up crated, gathering dust in some basement, so I said I would give them the show provided they would hang it," De Grazia explained. Since the University could not

20

come up with the permanent quarters for the paintings, the offer was withdrawn.

It is safe to assume, that the successful show at the University of Arizona was one of the sweeter moments in the artists life. Even today, after many years of success and adulation, De Grazia conceals his disappointment over the long period of non-acceptance with some difficulty. An understandable distrust of critics and the art establishment still remains.

Back in 1943, however, De Grazia was deeply hurt by the rebuff of the University where he had studied. Nonetheless he decided to complete his studies that he had broken off earlier. This time around he perservered and earned three degrees: Bachelor of Fine Arts in Art, Bachelor of Arts in Music Education and to top it all off, a Masters of Arts degree. So much for primitive! He wrote his thesis on the subject: "Art and its Relation to Music in Art Education." In this learned treatise De Grazia claims, ". . . Basically, music and painting are the same, the common root being emotion." And in a swipe at the art establishment, "Too many painters today have forgotten the important lesson, that true art is life-interpretation, not merely an exercise in technique."

De Grazia completed his academic education in 1945 and even taught art for one semester in a private school. All it taught him was that he was not cut out to be an educator. "It took too much out of me and my own painting suffered," he says.

Undaunted by the rejection of his work, he decided to go it alone. "None of the galleries wanted to show my work, so I decided to build my own gallery." With a little borrowed money he managed a down payment on a piece of bristly desert outside of Tucson and set to work. Collecting his materials from the desert around him, he and a few friends, mostly Mexicans and Indians, erected an adobe structure with window and door frames built from saguaro cactus spines. Ah, serenity! It was as if he had gathered up a piece of his beloved Arizona desert like a blanket and pulled it up over his life. Now he could paint seriously, to fill the walls of his own gallery.

The next few years were taken up with painting and extensive trips throughout Arizona and the jungles of Mexico. De Grazia roamed through Indian country and studied the early history of these regions. Submerging himself in the study of the lives of the

conquerors, the lore of the Papagos, Yaquis, the Apaches, Navajos and the Seri Indians, he became fascinated with the purity of life of these tribes before they were subjugated and changed. Needless to say, his art reflected these interests in extensive series of sketches and ultimately, groups of paintings.

De Grazia made his first trip to New York in 1947 and has made a few sporadic sorties outside of his magic circle since then. But recently he remarked, "There is no place I want to go any more, unless it is Indian country."

It was a productive time, but was it a happy one? He had created a lot of ceramics and paintings and had lined them up along the road in front of his studio. After an extended absence, he returned to find them undisturbed. "Nobody even bothered to steal them," De Grazia grumbled.

But his work, did that bring him happiness? When a guest asked him that, De Grazia replied, "I get lost in my work when I am painting and I don't know what happiness is."

Moreover, the city of Tucson drove him out of his gallery. The urban sprawl of the city had swallowed up what had been virginal desert, and De Grazia's gallery was suddenly surrounded by bustling suburbs, his studio on a busy intersection.

He felt an urgent need to remove himself from all that and in 1951 purchased a 10 acre parcel of desert land in the foothills of the Santa Catalina Mountains, then far outside the city limits.

24

"Yeibechai", Oil,
24 x 18, 1962

25

The first structure he built was a chapel in honor of the Virgin of Guadalupe. Erected with desert materials, the chapel has an open roof, to allow the elements to participate in whatever takes place there. It has a quiet dignity and one has the feeling that the Mother of God would be pleased with such a dwelling. The walls are covered with murals by De Grazia and at night, the stars shed a pale, gentle light on this humble offering.

The rest of the buildings on the property are rambling, low-slung adobe structures that hug the landscape and somehow do not disturb the balance of nature. They are modeled after the haciendas on the ranches of Mexico and "Arizona Highways" former editor Raymond Carlson once remarked, that the Gallery in the Sun and Frank Lloyd Wright's Taliesin West are the two pieces of architecture best adapted to the Arizona landscape.

27

The main room of the Gallery
in the Sun, Tucson.

Yaqui Deerdancer Bronze
statue tops a fountain in the
courtyard.

Amidst stands of cacti and a sprinkling of Palo Verde, the Gallery in the Sun is a sanctuary for De Grazia and also for his friends and visitors, who come from all parts of the world. The gallery itself has no windows because De Grazia feels that walls are for hanging paintings. Over the years the simple structure has sprawled with additions, adding more and more walls for De Grazia's work.

The year 1950 was significant for De Grazia in another way. A short time before, De Grazia met Buck Saunders, the owner of a newly opened art gallery in Scottsdale, near Phoenix. This meeting developed into a friendship and a lasting alliance between the two men.

On February 5, 1950 Saunders held a one-man show of the paintings of De Grazia, the first such show for both men in Scottsdale. The opening of the show was a matter of concern for both Saunders and De Grazia. Saunders had never arranged an event of this nature and De Grazia had not sold very many paintings.

On the eve of the opening, De Grazia repainted the walls of the gallery to show off his paintings to their best advantage. Saunders and a few helpers assisted in this last-minute endeavor. The most expensive price tag was $500 for an oil that would fetch in excess of $20,000 today, if it were available.

To everyone's amazement, more than 1,000 people crowded through the gallery and the neighboring bars and restaurants ran out of ice and food. Considering that the population of Scottsdale was little more than 2,000 in those days, it could be described as a smash hit.

When the evening was over, De Grazia had made his largest sale to date, $1,500 worth of paintings were snapped up.

In spite of tempting offers from other art dealers since then, De Grazia has remained loyal to the man who first believed in him. Buck Saunders still is the only gallery authorized to sell original oils by De Grazia. This is considered a rarity in the highly volatile marketplace of art and speaks well for this happy association. Even some of De Grazia's detractors, who like to accuse him of venality, are impressed by such loyalty.

Things began to look up considerably. In 1952 the tireless artist turned his hand to designing textiles and again travelled to New York for that venture. But De Grazia out of his own landscape is like a fish on dry land. He hurried back to the Southwest, his land, into the sun. Clearly, the sun is De Grazia's proper star, and his gallery in Tucson is therefore aptly named Gallery in the Sun. As he once pointed out: "We only have life because of the sun. I work in the sun, prospect in the sun, I have even made love in the sun. What other symbol could fit my gallery?"

And De Grazia basked in it throughout 1953, a year he described as the year of ING's: prospecting, painting, smoking. He had found his center at last, his equilibrium. Only a damn fool would step outside of that.

By then, the world who had spurned his efforts for so long, was beating a path to his door. De Grazia had become a painter at last, after all those years of searching and penury, of doubt and sweat.

He reflected on that long, thistly road recently, "When you have become a painter, you will have paid for it dearly. Not in money. The price comes out of your soul, you pay with your very hide." When an art student once asked how he could become a painter, De Grazia told him: "First you must grow a beard. Then you must wait for the beard to turn grey. And then — maybe! — you will become a painter."

Being fiercly independent himself, DeGrazia's fascination with the American Indians is quite natural. As a man of courage, he understands intuitively the heroism involved in their plight. To fight against impossible odds, to persist in a way of life that is clearly doomed by the overpowering onslaught of another time, must have a strong appeal to any sensitive person. The quiet dignity with which a large part of the population of an entire continent died, must have stirred the soul of the young painter.

Moreover, De Grazia understood so well the deep roots in the sun-parched earth that motivated these peoples. The simplicity and directness of their relationship with the environment was something starkly familiar to him.

Their land must have seemed to him like a Morenci with traditions and bonds. A homeland worth dying for.

In addition to that, what a contrast to the Anglos he knew in the mining community: driven by greed, eternal foreigners on the beautiful soil they tore up, worthy neither of emulation nor admiration. As he said: "The Indian story reads like an ancient parchment." There was the elegiac quality of an ode. Finally, they were also remarkable human beings with failings and charms. Colorful and full of surprises, they were picturesque.

Asked about that aspect of the Indians, De Grazia explains, "Papagos, Apaches, Yaquis. They are God's gift to painters. They are colorful, they have dignity, pride and respect. We work together, drink together and become friends. We stay together, we have many laughs. And now, we are growing old together."

Most of De Grazia's paintings mirror his love and concern for the Indians. Reverently, he records their rituals, depicts the delight he finds in the simplicity of their day-to-day life.

De Grazia with members of a Christmas carolling group.

What could be more moving than the children of such a race? Or, in his own words, "Children — they are all over my canvases. You see these beautiful black eyes looking at you with awe."

In 1960, UNICEF approached De Grazia for a painting which they could use on a Christmas card. He painted his best-known canvas for them: "Los Niños". Over five million boxes of this card were sold. The message inside was printed in English, Spanish, French, Russian and Chinese and they were sold the world over. UNICEF described the painting as, ". . . a sensitive and moving portrayal of Indian children performing a ceremonial dance."

More and more, De Grazia avoided painting in the faces of the figures in his subsequent paintings. In a sense, it made his people more universal, allowed the viewer to fill in his own choice of features. While most of the children in his work do have faces, they are so stylized that one is again free to interpret them.

Because of the unprecedented success of "Los Niños" and other paintings of children, De Grazia felt that he was in danger of being typecast as a chronicler of infants. "I had decided not to paint children again. But we went to Guatemala and there was a little girl of six or seven, standing on a corner, boiling coffee. Beautiful! I liked that beloved little kid and just had to paint little kids again," De Grazia said.

▶

"Los Niños", Oil, 24 x 26, 1957

"Merry Little Indian", Oil, 9 x 12, 1972

Over the years, he has donated more than $10 million in
originals and prints to various foundations and charities for children
such as the Cocopah's tribe ``Cry House'', the San Diego Children's
Hospital, the Arizona Boys' Ranch and many others.

In a sense, De Grazia identifies with his Indian friends and he is not happy with the changes he sees. "The Indians I know best are the Indians of my era — the long-haired ones. I respect them and they respect me," he said. And in the key of despair, almost like an old Chief, he adds, "Now this new generation of Indian appears on the horizon. This time irritated, in full regalia. He comes in a new car and with a wristwatch. He is over-exposed and over-talked-about. NO HORSE!"

Is this the end of the Indian? Of men like De Grazia? Not very likely. As for the Indians, their nobility will live on even if the tribal structure perishes. And De Grazia? As the noted critic Frank DeHoney once put it, "Nothing of his is a copy of any other style known. His individualism is unique and absolute . . . His impact will probably be felt for as long as our civilization survives."

Long forgotten are the years of poverty and struggle. The Gallery in the Sun flourishes and De Grazia has become a household word. His art seems to have struck a chord in the hearts of a large number of people of the most diverse backgrounds. His images are distributed in a multitude of forms. Prints, serigraphs, decals, collector plates, needlepoint, cards, books and even keychains. There is a groundswell of enthusiasm for his work almost with the force of a religion.

De Grazia likes the idea of all these reproductions spread around, likes knowing that his public can buy prints for a few dollars if they want them. To him, that is better than a coterie of investors who outbid each other for rare originals.

The high priests of the art world are disturbed by this unorthodox behavior. It is apparently perfectly acceptable for an artist to starve, but one with a cash register at the end of his counter is considered an anathema. What is held to be virtuous in an accountant or stockbroker, somehow becomes despicable in a creative person.

Perhaps the critics cannot forgive that he became successful not only without their help and approval, but also despite their indifference. They now accuse him of selling out, because his work has such wide appeal. They call him an art factory, because he is so prolific; some even have hinted darkly, that someone else — a group perhaps — produces all of his work and he merely signs it.

De Grazia bears these attacks with equanimity. Whenever his enfant-terrible behavior draws censure, he shrugs, "I would rather be notorious than famous. Fame brings too many responsibilities. People forget that you are human."

38

Success seems not to have spoiled DeGrazia. He uses a better grade snuff than in the old days, drinks Scotch instead of mescal and corn liquor of the lean years. Other than that, he appears unchanged. His only concession to affluence is a sleek, white Mercedes, which purrs and is fleet of wheel. The reason for that could well be, that it gets him back home faster, whenever he has to go up to Phoenix on business.

There is now an air of wisdom about him, an absence of chaos. After long hours of work he may occasionally show a touch of weariness, but through it shimmers a balance of inner peace. He still does not suffer fools too gladly, but more patiently. And he seems to have preserved his capacity for wonder and enthusiasm.

Watching him deal with visitors to his gallery, with his staff or his friends, one is struck by the respect he shows them all, by the lack of scorn in his mien.

39

*De Grazia and Bernardino, his
Yaqui Deerdancer friend.*

*De Grazia and
his friend
"Two-Guns".*

Among his friends, there are two who work for him, doing odd jobs around the gallery. A gentle, sunny Anglo, aptly nicknamed "Two-Guns", who dreams of landing a role in a Western movie and is always on call. Meanwhile, he is in costume around the clock, carrying two large colts in a clanking holster and a marvelous cowboy hat with considerably more character than substance.

Two-Guns can be seen most days walking through the gallery in a colorful poncho, spurs a-tinkle, on his way to paint some floor tiles in a new wing. He spins around at any challenge from behind a post, ready to draw, and he is proud of the fact, that he does all his own stunts.

Another employee claims that Two-Guns lives in a time-warp, oblivious to the fact, that the West is not so Wild any more. De Grazia delights in the purity of Two-Guns' fantasies and horses around with him a lot. Yet, he never ridicules him.

The other friend is a Yaqui Indian deerdancer, Bernardino Valencia, of indeterminate age, a gifted musician, who plays flute and a hand drum simultaneously, in the Yaqui manner. Bernardino looks after the grounds and has done so for the last eight years or so.

There is such an innocence about Bernardino, that it tends to humble visiting cynics. He smiles a lot and is happy and De Grazia loves him like a son.

Not only does De Grazia pose as the caretaker on the telephone, but as a ranchhand at gas stations; or as a cowpoke to car salesmen, who then try to sell him the cheapest heap in the lot. If people recognize him, fine. If not, fine also. His people, his army of admirers sense this humility in him and they like it.

His notoriety allows him to remain human, as he has said. Has his success gone to his head? When a guest asked him about that recently, he scratched his forehead for a spell and then answered, "You know, it is a funny thing about having success as a painter. When you start out, nobody believes in you but yourself. After you have finally made it, everybody believes in you, but you yourself have your doubts."

*Bernardino provides Yaqui
Indian music in the gallery on
festive occasions.*

It is 4:00 p.m. and De Grazia is about to close shop and vanish for the remainder of the day. This a good point to end our quest and it is only fitting, to let our subject have the last word. He wrote it at the end of a biographical timetable. After the last entry, having said everything he was willing to say, he wrote in large letters:

"EVERYBODY GO HOME!"

Part Two

THE MAN AND HIS MOUNTAIN

By Harry Redl

46

"To me, the Superstition Mountain
is full of mystery and intrigue. She is
the most beautiful mountain in the
whole world. At times she looks old,
very very old, craggy and tired, and
very sad. Yet at other times she looks
young and lovely
. . . You too will fall in love with
her . . . Soon you will succumb to her
and she will possess you completely."

Ted De Grazia

East of Phoenix, near the desert town of Apache Junction, Arizona, an awesome mountain range suddenly rears out up out of the cacti and gallops on into the distance like a wild bronco. It is an immense expanse of rock. Nothing seems easier than to become hopelessly lost in its bounding lines of peaks, its maze of canyons, and indeed, many men have disappeared there over the years.

These are the Superstition Mountains, legendary to the Indians as well as to the Spaniards, and all those who came after them.

The fabled Lost Dutchman Mine, presumably a rich lode of gold, is thought to be buried under tons of boulders in the wake of an earthquake that shook the land in 1887. When the Jesuit padres who had arrived with the Conquistadores, were about to be replaced by Franciscan fathers in 1764, the Jesuits are said to have gathered all their valuables from the Missions of southern Arizona and northern Mexico. The forlorn caravan was seen riding into the mountains and coming out empty of their load. This treasure of gold, ornaments and religious artifacts, such as golden chalices, silver candelabras and the like, is probably buried somewhere around Weaver's Needle, a monolithic rock outcropping in one of the wide valleys.

Scores of wild-eyed fortune-hunters have combed the Superstitions' reaches since then. None have unearthed them so far, but many of the searchers have perished under mysterious circumstances.

The mountains reputedly house a tribe of Little People, an Arizona version of the Wee Folk of Ireland. From the Maricopa Indians stems the legend of the Stone People, irreverent folk who mocked their gods and wound up forming the crest of a ridge, petrified and sorrow-bent. Aside from this population, any number of less exotic ghosts haunt the Superstitions. But more than anything, the mountains reek of gold.

De Grazia is the Superstitions' most illustrious lover and has celebrated their charms in drawings, paintings and prose poems. It could well be, that these mountains are the essence of all that is dear to him.

49

a midnight sketch JAN 24 DeGrazia Arizona 1972

Indian lore abounds there. De Grazia's trusted companion, the sun, parches its ridges during the summer, and there is metal underfoot. There, you can get on a horse and chase the javelino, the pygmy wild pig of the Southwest. There you can be free. And with a lot of hard work, with a little luck, you could come away with a treasure.

De Grazia understands the smoldering dreams of the prospectors, because he is one of them. He, too, is looking for the pot of gold, is panning for the nuggets of truth and beauty with his sketches. Moreover, he has spent many hours digging in the mountains for the real gold as well. His longings are similar to those of the full-time free-booters on their burros.

In a book first published by himself and later by the University of Arizona Press in 1972, titled: *The Superstition: De Grazia and His Mountain,* the artist wrote the following passage, perhaps more than a little autobiographical:

THE PROSPECTOR

"The prospector is a rare individual. He prefers to live alone, far away from civilization, far away alone with nature. His needs are few. He can get by with very little — almost nothing.

The prospector has become a symbol — an old man with a beard, a white beard, alone with his trusted burro. He disappears over the horizon into the mountains, always to follow the rainbow, seeking the pot of gold.

Every day brings new hope. He thinks that Lady Luck, maybe this time, will smile on him and present him with a ledge of gold — a bonanza!

He spends all his waking hours roaming the hills, looking for a place rich in pay dirt. When he finds a place that looks like that, he settles down for some serious digging — trying here and there.

He digs and digs and digs, hoping to find the vein of gold. The prospector has left many a hole in the mountain as he disappears over the horizon.

The prospector was once a young man with a black beard. But the days have gone into weeks, weeks into months, months into years — into many many years. Now he is old and his body bent. He looks toward his mountain, and he still daydreams. He is sad. There is no place for him on his mountain anymore. He longs for one more glipmse of gold — one glimpse of the mountain's richness. He is still a little man, with only a burro, who has pointed the way for others who are waiting and ready to grasp his gold.

He is alone again.

Ted De Grazia

53

The "Dutchman" of the legend, really a German named Jacob Walz, was such a prospector, who found his pot of gold at the end of the rainbow. His story, or rather the gist of the many versions of it, reads like a morality play. Greed for gold brings death and destruction. But Jacob Walz was a kindly man, who understood the nature of mountains and of gold and De Grazia has this to say about him:

"I believe that the Dutchman was a man of great capacity, a man deeply sad and alone, a man who realized the responsibility of the possession of gold, a man of great understanding. He knew where the gold was. Yet he left it where it was and tapped it only for his humble needs. He didn't gouge the mountain and rob her of her gold.

. . . I believe the Dutchman knew the value of gold, but he also knew that gold was a means to an end. Gold was not to be used in a vulgar way, for power, or to display wealth.

Gold has to be used in an humble way, with respect and only when needed.

Ted De Grazia

The true prospector, De Grazia is saying, has a deep respect for his mountain. He will not pillage boundlessly, but will only nourish himself. The Indians used to hunt buffalo this way until the White man introduced deadly method into this holy ritual.

There are certain ground rules to the game of life, not to be broken without serious consequences. Any mountain will endure goodnaturedly, a certain amount of digging; she will feed you graciously. If violated, she will defend her treasures ferociously.

In the 1970's, De Grazia became aware of an injustice, which, in his eyes, represented just such a gouging. This time, not of a mountain by a prospector, but of all the artists by the Government of the United States.

54

a midnight sketch
Arizona
1972

Under tax laws passed in 1969, the estate of a deceased artist would be taxed on the market value of the works of art passed on to the heirs. If the artist, however, wanted to donate his works to a charitable cause during his lifetime, the Internal Revenue Department would allow a tax deduction based on the value of the materials only.

De Grazia was shocked to read the case of the famous sculptor David Smith. Smith, reluctant to part with his enormous metal-sculptures, had accumulated a large yard full of his sought-after pieces. Upon Smith's death, his family was presented with an inheritance tax bill of over $2 million. Unable to meet such an obligation, the government settled for $250,000 and part of future royalties on the sculptor's work.

It seemed to De Grazia, that the family literally had to buy back the work of their family head from a rapacious taxman.

To compound the offensiveness of this tax law, the government ignored the market value of the artworks when it would have been advantageous to the living artist.

De Grazia was furious: "If anyone else buys my painting for $2, he can then give it to a museum and deduct $10,000 from his taxes, if that is the market value of the piece. If I myself donate it, I get $2 tax credit, because that is what the paint and the canvas cost."

The final disenchantment came, when De Grazia read about the death of the cartoonist Walt Kelly, the creator of Pogo. His family literally faced bankruptcy, when the inheritance tax bill arrived.

De Grazia has kept most of his oils over the years and he realized he could not afford to die. It would spell ruin to his heirs.

Slowly his anger became a roar and in 1976, he decided, that in a desperate gesture of protest, he would destroy some of his work. No government could prevent him from doing that. Let the museums gasp and groan.

Photos by Paul DeGruccio

In May 1976, De Grazia burned $1.5 million of his works at Angel Springs, deep in the Superstition Mountains.

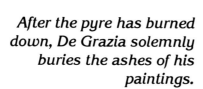

After the pyre has burned down, De Grazia solemnly buries the ashes of his paintings.

58

And this is the point, where the metaphorical mountain ends and the real Superstitions come in again.

De Grazia had written about the real mountain:

"In spite of the hardships and frightening experiences, I will return again to this mountain, for there I have found beauty, exhilarating visions of nature's creations.

Others before me must have experienced the same feeling. The names they left behind tell me so. In this mountain they have found the Prayer Room, Angel Springs, and the Sacred Caves. And there is the Madonna of the Mountain.

One little prospector left behind a peach tree and a rose bush. But none are able to contribute much to this mountain."

A few packhorses joined the ride into the Superstitions, when De Grazia and a party of ten friends and observers saddled up somberly for that long climb on May 12, 1976.

The grizzled prospector was on his way to his mountain again. This time to pay homage. This time with a sacrifice.

Grimly, the party headed for Angel Springs, deep in the creeks of the mountainfolds, between Roger Canyon and Goat Canyon.

There, the old prospector built a funeral pyre for his niños. He piled over 150 paintings and other works helter-skelter, straight up. And with tears running down his face, he put a match to this pyramid of dreams. Under the watchful eyes of the Stone People, the Little People, the ghosts of Padre Kino, the Jesuit padres; with the hollow eyes of the Dutchman's spirit and those of all the fortune hunters who died among these boulders looking on silently, De Grazia watched his treasure turn to ashes.

It was a widely talked-about action and De Grazia received mail from as far away as England, sympathizing with his point of view.

There were those who accused him of seeking publicity. But if that had been his motivation, it would have been more effective to send his work up in smoke outside of the Federal Building or even his Tucson studio.

In his anger, De Grazia vowed never to paint another canvas. There was no way to redeem the burnt works, but that vow eventually had to be broken. After all, how long can a man hold his breath?

After a 3-year hiatus, De Grazia started painting oils again. All the canvases he produced after that fateful day at Angel Springs, bear a serial number on the back. Next to the number, De Grazia writes the initials "A.B."

They stand for: After Burning.

a midnight sketch winter 44 in
DeGrazia Arizona 1972
USA

"Alone", Oil,
10 x 18, 1964

62

De Grazia and his Mountain are on the best of terms now. Whenever the spirit moves him, when the pressures of the Gallery would become too much for him, he heads for the Superstition. To recharge his batteries, as he says.

Nowadays, he comes as a friend and lover. No more lonely gropings under the rocks, no solitary burro tagging along with pans and picks.

Just a crystalline serenity that pervades the craggy canyons and fills his soul with new hope.

What a joy to ride on the trails where all his fascinating predecessors had gone towards their separate destinies. All one has to do is close one's eyes for a moment to hear the cries of Peralta's muleteers, the whoops of the Apaches, the groans of the lonely men in search of gold.

And high above the ridges, in the deep blue of the southwestern skies, the hawks fly their lazy, watchful circles.

What better place could there be for a man to be alone with his thoughts?

63

De Grazia likes to take his friends into the Mountain, to show them the regal beauty of his beloved.

When he went up to Weaver's Needle recently, six other riders and a ranchhand in charge of the horses went with him. His 70-odd years notwithstanding, De Grazia mounted his steed swiftly and led the group up the canyon.

Almost imperceptibly the grade steepened and the horses dug their hooves into the narrow pathway at a steady pace.

After crossing some verdant washes, the column emerged from the vegetation and entered the arid crevices of the mountain itself.

The change in mood was almost palpable. As the path wound up into the walls of rock, De Grazia became looser and more flexible with each step.

He told his companions the Legend of the Stone People as the party passed the mountain ridge that looks like a thousand sad, hunched-over figures crouching in the sun.

The Maricopa Indians passed this tale on to their children, when they wondered at the oddly shaped ridges that cap some of the peaks.

It seems that the Earth Doctor had made people out of clay, but had forgotten an important ingredient: the spirit of kindness and love. They turned out mean and cantankerous and they displeased the Earth Doctor so much, that he told the dreamy moon and the yellow sun to go away for forty days.

It rained and the valleys flooded. Then it rained some more and the mean people were driven to the pinnacle of the mountain where they froze and turned into stone. A grim reminder of the vicissitudes of human frailty.

67

69

70

On top of the steep climb, there is a sudden vista of the Weaver's Needle soaring from the sole of the valley, so breathtaking that even the horses seem to break their gait.

They had arrived. This was the vantage point the painter had in mind to show them.

The party dismounted and now that the noises of the journey had ceased, silence fell on them like an Indian blanket. It was too awesome to talk and the riders silently wandered along the edge of the plateau.

De Grazia, with a smile, downed a sandwich, broke the seal on a whiskey bottle and settled on a ledge to survey the panorama. It is a familiar scene to him, to be sure. But it never looks quite the same as the last time.

Then he pulled out his notebook and his nimble pen started to sketch the rock and the slanting shadows that furrow the valley.

Far away a column of smoke.

Peace.

71

Part Three

THE PAINTINGS

A portfolio of 62 oils
by Ted De Grazia 1925-1980

The following 62 canvases are a unique group of paintings. Mr. De Grazia was asked to pick them out of his large body of work. This is tantamount to asking the head of a large family to pick his favorite child. It is very likely that at another time, the artist would choose another group altogether.

These oils stem from the years 1925 to 1980 and thus afford us a rare look at a lifetime of painting.

"4 Horses", Oil,
18 x 18, 1925

24 x 16, 1925

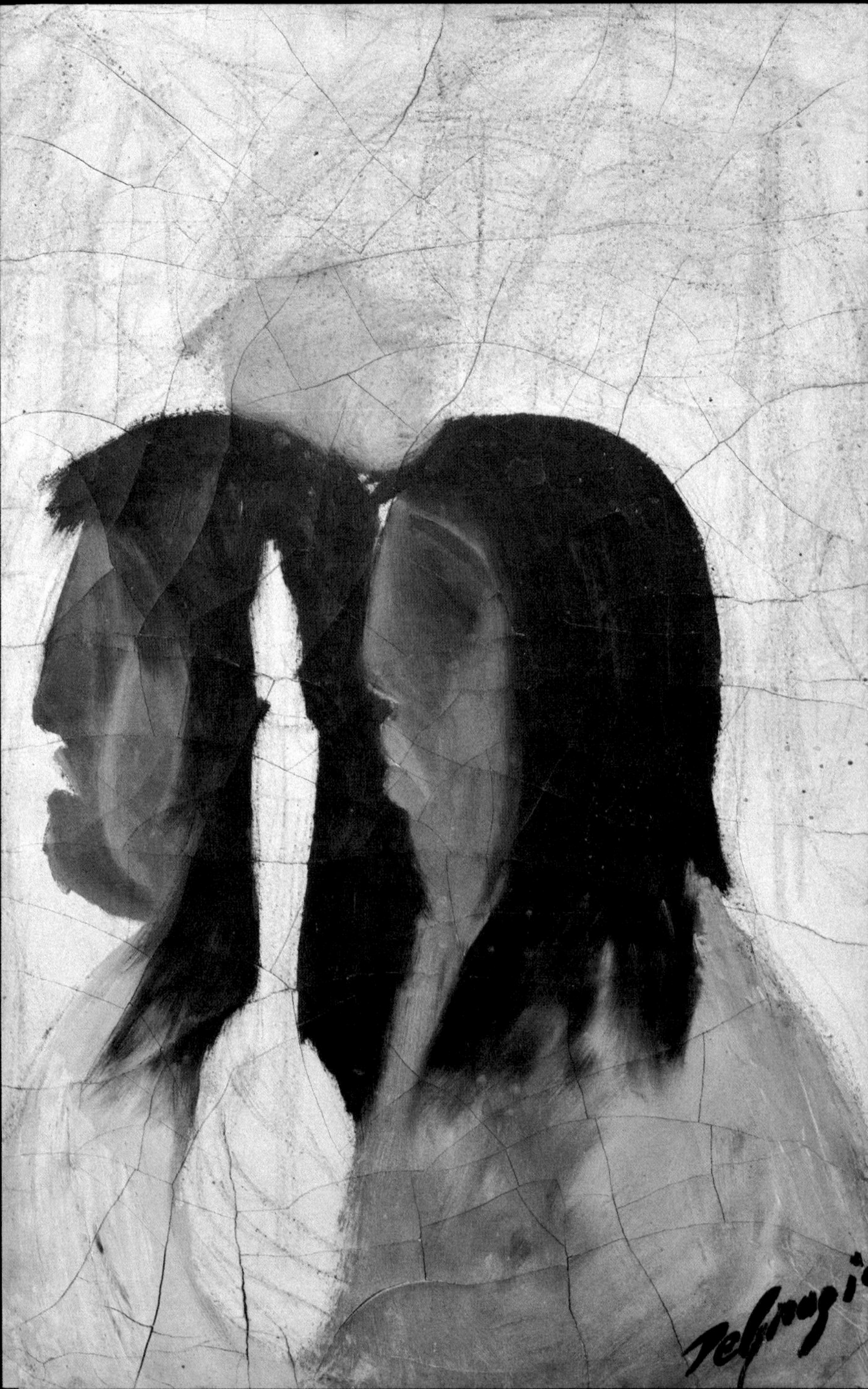

"Mexicanos", Oil,
30 x 20, 1940

"Viva", Oil,
30 x 24, 1940

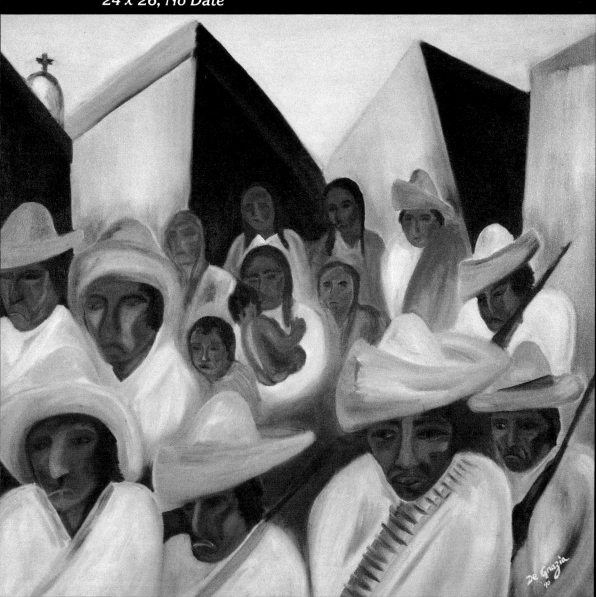

"Huelga", Oil,
24 x 26, No Date

"*Perdidos*", Oil,
26 x 32, 1941

"Defeat", Oil,

"Prayers", Oil,
26 x 20, 1941

"Skipping Rope", Oil,
30 x 24, 1941

"Fiesta Time", Tempera
36 x 20, 1942

85

*"Tears for a Dead Child", Oil,
24 x18, 1942*

"Head of Christ", Oil,
24 x18, 1942

"With Basket on Head", Oil,
20 x 14, 1947

"Two Bathers",

*"Ferdinand Schoville's
Beggar", Oil,
14 x 24, 1948*

"Mother and Daughter",
Oil, 1948

"Performing Clown", Oil,
16 x 20, 1948

"Ranchita", Oil,
24 x 16, 1948

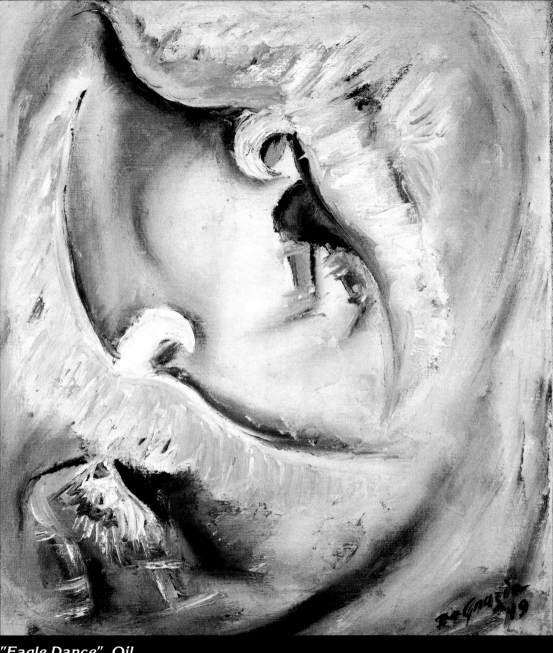

"Eagle Dance", Oil,
20 x 18, 1949

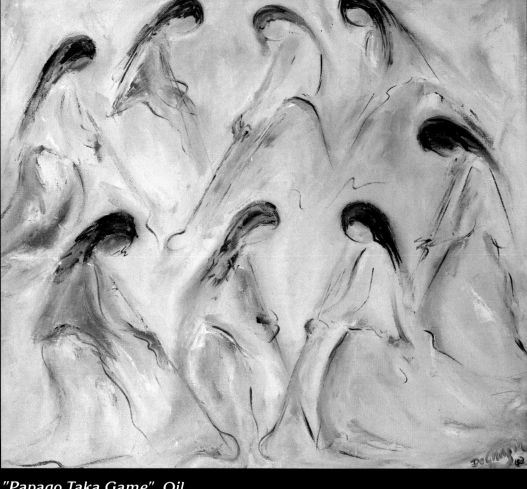

"Papago Taka Game", Oil,
28 x 32, 1950

"Dancing Ballerina",
Oil, 1951

"Clowns", Oil,

"Unnamed",
Oil on Wood Panel, 1953

"Love that Watermelon", Oil,
26 x 30, 1954

16 x 22, 1955

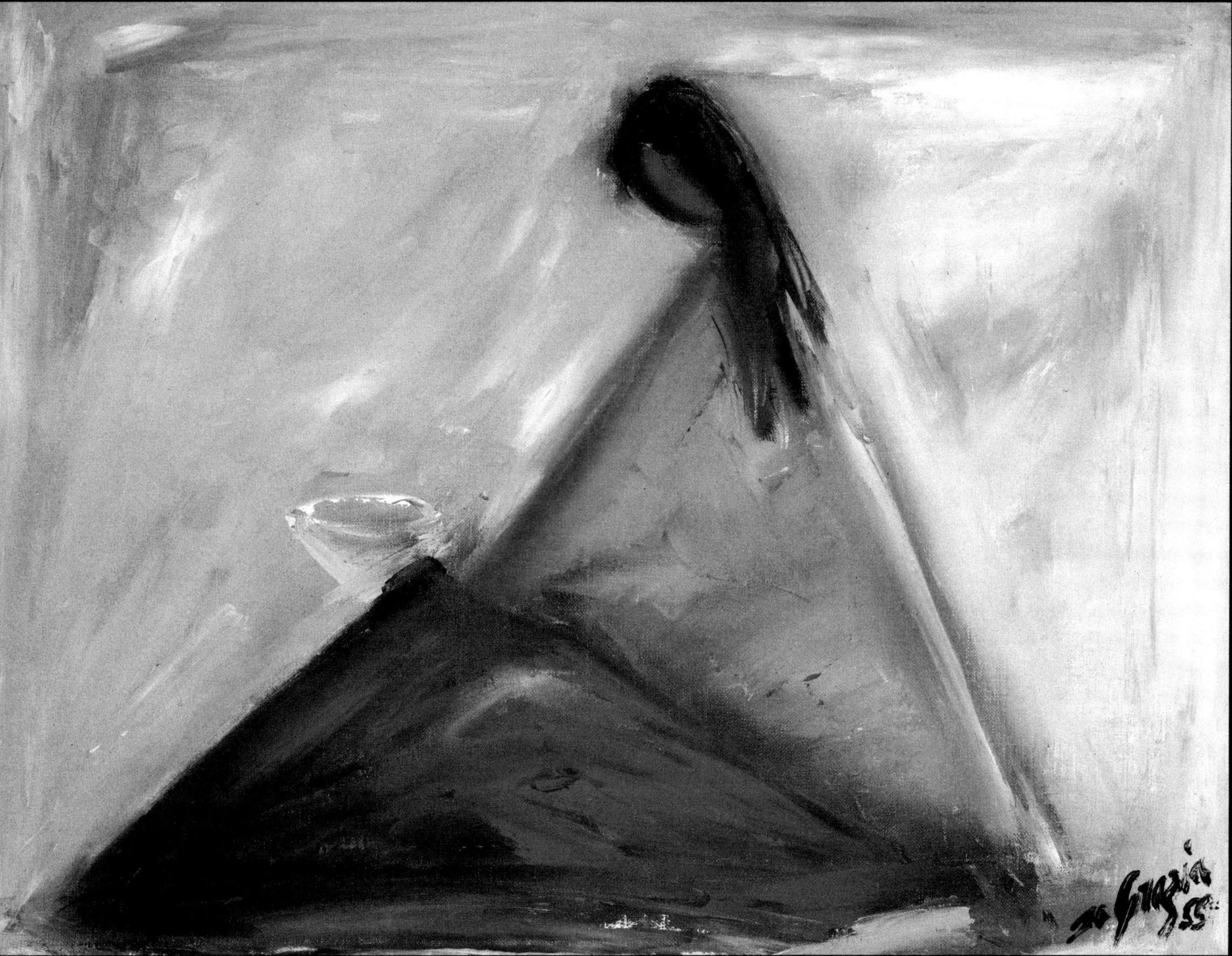

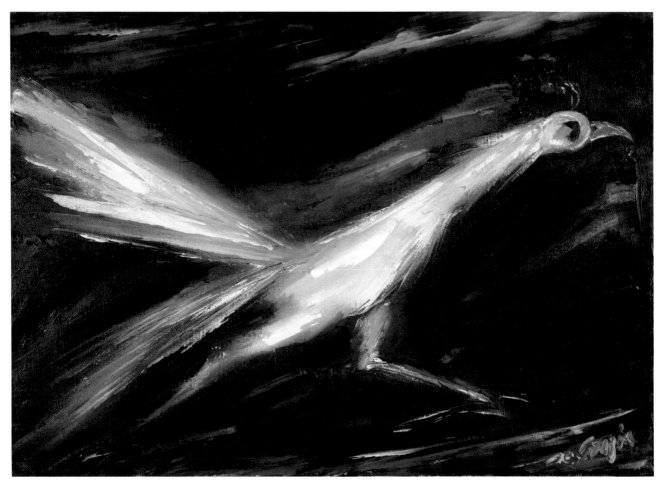

"Midnight Road Runner", Oil,
14 x 20, 1956

102

"Beggar and Musician", Oil,
24 x16, 1955

"Midnight Angel Variation",
Oil, 26 x 20, 1956

104

"Bucking Bronco", Oil,
12 x 14, 1956

"Three Horses from the Last",
Oil, 16 x 24, 1956

106

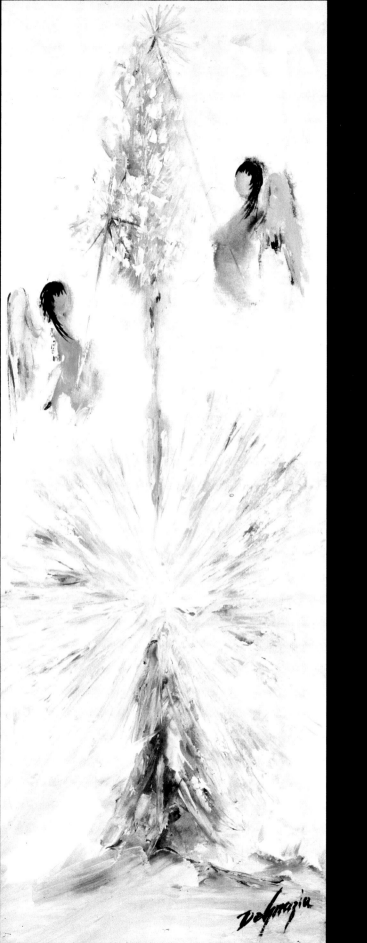

"Two Angels Lighting the Lords Candle", *Oil,*
24 x 9, No Date

"Los Niños", Oil,
24 x 26, 1957

"Mexican Bar Scene",
Oil, 15 x 22, 1957

110

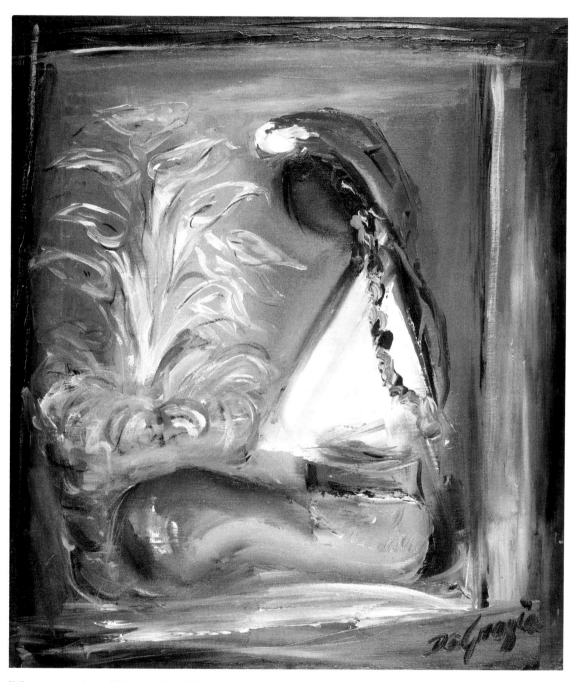

"Guatemalan Woman", Oil,
18 x 16, 1958

"Young Hoop Dancer",
Oil, 26 x 24, 1958

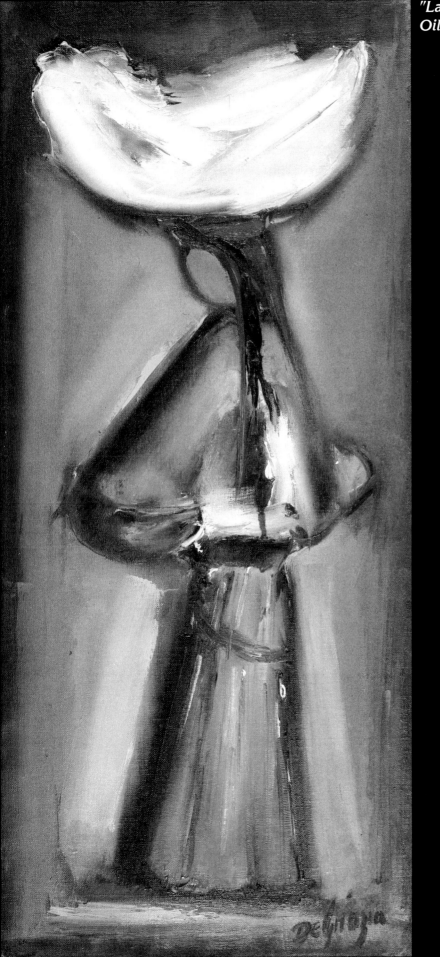

"Meditation in Red", Oil,
20 x11, 1959

"Revolution", Oil,
30 x 38, 1959

"Padre Kino Enters Altar Valley",
Oil, 26 x 20, 1960

DeGrazia

"Hoop Dancer", Oil,
24 x18, 1962

"Yeibechai", Oil,
24 x 18, 1962

"Waiting", Oil,
12 x18, 1962

"Morning Ride", Oil,
20 x 14, 1963

"This Day", Oil,
14 x 20, 1963

122

"Alone", Oil,
10 x18, 1964

"For the Fire of Life", Oil,
20 x 12, 1965

"Selfportrait", Oil,
18 x 14, 1965

125

"El Metate", Oil,
6 x 8, 1965

126

"Festival of Lights", Oil,
20 x 14, 1965

"One Slice", Oil,
8 x18, 1970

"Merrily, Merrily, Merrily. . ."
Oil, 7½ x 9½, 197

*"Merry Little Indian", Oil,
9 x 12, 1972*

"Baptism Papoose",
Oil, 16 x 8, 1974

133

De Grazia

"La Pinata", Oil
5 x 7, 1965

"Christmas Angels"
Oil, 5 x 7, 1980

136

Part Four

THE MAN AND HIS ART

by Buck Saunders

a midnight sketch

June 18

1968

Every successful artist must have an individual style. Ted De Grazia has one so dramatically his own, it is recognized around the world.

De Grazia developed that style after years of searching for the best means to express his personal, mystical impressions of the people and elements in the great American Southwest and Mexico. Now, so true to intent is his technique that people everywhere respond to his paintings freely, unanalytically. His images hold unwavering appeal because his meaning is immediately understandable, never disguised. De Grazia says, "It's not how much paint from the tube I put on the canvas, or even how much I leave out. I work for the *feeling* of a piece."

Although his work is instantly recognizable, it is not easily labeled. No one art world formula can explain this creative and multi-talented artist. He is an Impressionist; he is an Expressionist. He is a Realist, but not one whose work mimics photography. He is a Romantic; his art, a piquant combination of naiveté and sophistication. More spontaneous than intellectual, the "De Grazia Style" is beyond time and space. It is visionary fabrication drawn from the inner depths of the man himself.

How De Grazia came to his visual language is a study in many volumes. He has progressed from a style closely allied with the work of artists he admired to his own special look.

Those artists whose influence can be seen in his early work are El Greco, Paul Gauguin, Georges Rouault, Vincent Van Gogh, José Clemente Orozco and Diego Rivera.

De Grazia made a pilgrimage to Tahiti to experience first-hand the area where Gauguin worked, and in the early 1940s he studied in Mexico City with Orozco and Rivera, working with them on the murals they created for the Palace of Fine Arts. These two giants in Mexican art, in fact, predicted the success De Grazia would later achieve, and encouraged him by sponsoring an exhibition of his work at the Palace in November of 1942.

De Grazia began developing his technique while studying with Rivera and Orozco and spent the next ten years refining it. But technique was always less interesting to him than the emotion he wished to portray.

141

The early oil paintings by De Grazia were done with a brush. For the past thirty years he has worked almost exclusively with a palette knife, using a brush only to achieve special effects. De Grazia has become a master in using the knife as a painting tool, and his work can be either smooth or have a build-up of paint with an impasto effect. What finally has become his hallmarks, however, are the way he paints faces, and his very sensitive use of color.

Until 1948 — with a few exceptions during the mid 1940's, — De Grazia painted features on his subjects' faces. Since that year, he has practically eliminated all facial features on adults in his paintings, and used only small dots for the eyes and mouth on children. Often he omits even those meager indications of features on all but one or two faces in a group of children. His only exception to this technique is for historical portraits which he paints, for lack of any records, from his own impressions of how his subjects would have looked.

De Grazia works with only seven colors: brown, black, vermilion, blue and what he calls lemon-yellow, orange-yellow and brown-yellow. He uses his color for maximum drama and emotional appeal.

De Grazia is undoubtedly one of the most reproduced American artists. Some one hundred million of his images have been circulated throughout the world.

He first gained national recognition in 1958 when Hallmark used one of his paintings on a card. His single best-known painting is "Los Niños", created in 1960 and selected by UNICEF for use on one of its holiday cards, which sold by the millions for several years. The image has since been reproduced on other greeting cards, in large prints, in stained glass and on the first in a popular series of collector plates now being made from De Grazia's paintings.

The first of two series of collector plates, decorated with reproductions of paintings by De Grazia, was started in late 1975 with the issue of the first in the "Children Series" the 1976 "Los Niños" plate. The first plate in the "Holiday Series" was the 1976 "Festival of Lights" plate. There will be ten plates in each series, one being issued each year for each series, and both series will end with the 1985 plate.

The Collector Plates:

All Plates Size 10¼"

1976 Los Niños,
Gorham,
Edition: 5,000
Children Series

1976 "Festival of Lights",
Fairmont,
Edition: 10,000
Holiday Series

1977 "The White Dove",
Gorham,
Edition: 10,000
Children Series

1977 "Bell of Hope",
Fairmont,
Edition: 10,000
Holiday Series

1978 "Flower Girl",
Fairmont,
Edition: 10,000
Children Series

1978 "Little Madonna",
Fairmont,
Edition: 10,000
Holiday Series

1979 "Flower Boy",
Fairmont,
Edition: 10,000
Children Series

1979 "The Nativity",
Artists of the World,
Edition: 10,000
Holiday Series

1980 "Little Cocopah Indian Girl",
Artists of the World,
Edition: 10,000
Children Series

1980 "Little Pima Indian
Drummer Boy",
Artists of the World,
Edition: 10,000
Holiday Series

1981 "Beautiful Burden",
Artists of the World,
Edition: 10,000
Children Series

1981 "A Little Prayer:
The Christmas Angel",
Artists of the World,
Edition: 10,000
Holiday Series

1982
"Merry Little Indian",
Artists of the World",
Edition: 10,000
Children Series

1982
"Blue Boy",
Artists of the World,
Edition: 10,000
Holiday Series

1983 "Wondering",
Artists of the World,
Edition: 10,000
Children Series

1983 "Heavenly Blessings",
Artists of the World,
Edition: 10,000
Holiday Series

1984 "The Pink Papoose",
Artists of the World,
Edition: 10,000
Children Series

1984 "Navajo Madonna",
Artists of the World,
Edition: 10,000
Holiday Series

1985
"Sunflower Boy",
Artists of the World,
Edition: 10,000
Children Series

1985
"Saguaro Dance",
Artists of the World,
Edition: 10,000
Holiday Series

Courtesy: Artists of the World, Inc.,
Scottsdale, Arizona.

147

"Seri Indian", Oil, 1969.

Because of those reproductions, he is probably best known for his paintings of children which, no matter what nationality De Grazia gave them, appear to viewers — regardless of their own background — as universal and personally recognizable. But De Grazia's subjects are many: Indian myths and legends, Christian and pagan religion, historical events and people, the rodeo and many similarly colorful features of the American Southwest.

De Grazia has become the foremost interpreter of the legends and myths of the Indian tribes in Arizona, New Mexico and Mexico. He has many friends among the Indians and visits them with an observing eye and a sympathetic ear. His paintings share with us his impressions of the Indian's religious life through the ceremonies he has witnessed, and the mythical figures he has imagined from the legends told to him by tribal elders. Many of these works have been published in books.

De Grazia Paints the Yaqui Easter was published in 1968 by the University of Arizona Press. This book features forty paintings interpreting Yaqui celebrations through each day of Lent. It shows the many parts of these neither Christian nor pagan celebrations and is, to me, an outstanding collection of De Grazia's work.

De Grazia usually exhibits this group of paintings in his Gallery in the Sun during the forty days of Lent.

De Grazia has visited the near-extinct Seri Indians in the Kino Bay area of northern Mexico many times. His impressions of the tribe are recorded in a number of paintings and sketches. Of note are his paintings showing the Seri women's almost lost custom of painting geometric designs on their faces. Because of their long friendship with De Grazia, the Seris painted their faces and allowed him to sketch them. This collection was used to illustrate a book written by William Neil Smith and published in 1970 under the title, *The Seri Indians, A Primitive People of Tiburon Island in the Gulf of California.*

In 1975 De Grazia completed a collection on his neighbors to the South: The Papago Indians who live in both Arizona and Mexico. The paintings portray the Papago's legends and myths and their past and present life styles. Many of them are included in the book, published that same year, *De Grazia Paints the Papago Indian Legends.* "Ho'ok, the Witch" from this collection has been

reproduced as a print, and in 1980 De Grazia cast an impressive bronze of this figure.

De Grazia was born and spent a large part of his youth in Morenci, adjacent to the San Carlos Apache reservation. His admiration for the Apache people led to a collection of sketches and paintings about their life, and especially their creation myths. These are included in his 1976 book, *De Grazia Paints the Apache Indians,* subtitled *And Myths of the Chiricahua Apaches, Son of Lightning, Culture Hero.* Of particular interest are the paintings "Apache Mother", "Apache Camp", "Crown Dancer" and "Raiding for Horses".

Much of his art — paintings and sculpture — is based on Christian religion. He is known, too, for his renderings of events historically important to the Southwest. The work comes only from De Grazia's long and serious study of history and the gift of his rich imagination; there are no neatly filed records on which to build his images.

The strongest of De Grazia's religious paintings are contained in a series called "The Way of the Cross". While most churches depict fourteen Stations of the Cross, De Grazia decided to add a fifteenth, "The Resurrection", for Easter. "Jesus Dies Upon the Cross", is one of the most stirring crucifixion renderings I have ever seen. Its fiery red background intensifies the figure of Christ slumped on the Cross and commands the viewer's attention.

The series hung for three years in the St. Thomas More Chapel at the Newman Center of the University of Arizona and during Easter this collection is on exhibit at the Gallery in the Sun.

De Grazia's talent and imagination as both painter and historian is much evident in the work he bases on events and people of years long past. With powerful use of line and color, he transports us through time. Some of these paintings also have been published in books.

150

From "The Way of the Cross",
Station XII — Jesus Dies
Upon the Cross

a midnight sketch 4 AM
JANUARY of 1973 DeGrazia
ARIZONA
U.S.A

A volume entitled *The Rose and The Robe; The Travels and Adventures of Fray Junipero Serra in California 1769-1784* was published in 1968. The work commemorates the bicentennial of Serra's founding of Christian missions along the California coast. A remarkable painting in this collection is "The Rose of Castile."

Several of his pen and ink studies for the Serra paintings were published in another book by De Grazia in 1969. It is entitled, *Father Junipero Serra; Sketches of His Life in California.*

In 1973 he published *De Grazia Paints Cabeza de Vaca.*

This volume describes the wanderings of the Spaniard Cabeza de Vaca and his group of men through the unmapped wild country towards Mexico City. Survivors of a shipwreck, these were the first non-Indians in Texas, New Mexico and Arizona.

The Spaniards were first prisoners, then slaves to the same Indians, which later assisted them and accompanied them on their trek through often unfriendly Indian country.

A strong and important work by De Grazia is his painting, "Padre Kino Enters Altar Valley", published in *De Grazia and Kino* in 1979. The book includes his complete twenty-piece portfolio on the Jesuit priest who traveled Northern Mexico and Southern Arizona establishing missions among the Indians. De Grazia began the series in 1961 and some of the paintings were reproduced in "Arizona Highways" magazine that year; he completed the collection in 1962.

Anyone who thinks De Grazia paints only cherubs and sweet-faced children would do well to look at the paintings in his book, *De Grazia and His Mountain, The Superstition,* published in 1972. Those who study his work will find special interest in this collection because of his inclusion of facial features in some of the paintings.

De Grazia has had a lifelong love of these Central Arizona mountains of mystery. The lure of gold in their rugged interior has drawn countless adventurers into their center and brought many to sorrow. De Grazia's fascination for those people linked to the numerous tales of the Superstitions are dramatically portrayed in this book. His inspiration for these paintings was born of curiosity and reverence from his close study of historical records on the mountains and his own trips into them.

"Cave Drawings",
Ceramic Plate, 17"

"Lonely Ride",
Ceramic Plate, 10', 1966

154

It is appropriate that De Grazia is best known for his paintings since most of his prodigious production has been in that medium, but there are few artistic media he has not tried over his half-century career.

In the later part of the 1940s De Grazia devoted most of his time to the creation and the production of ceramics. This enabled him to make a living from his creativity and allowed him to have some time to do that which he wanted most to do, paint. He created beautiful plates, bowls, figures and other pieces, which he decorated with brilliantly colored, hand-applied glazes.

On the plates he would often paint animals, clowns, and other things, such as the ancient symbols of the Hohokam Indians, and anything that his fertile imagination would dictate. He would often use commercial tile on which he would paint complete pictures in mosaic fashion. His ceramics were very popular, and are much sought after by collectors today.

During those years he created an enormous number of oils and watercolors, and his approach to painting was as individual as his art. He would stretch several canvases of various shapes and sizes and then hang them around his studio. As an idea came to him, he would pick an appropriate shape and sketch in a charcoal outline of the proposed painting. When he had several canvases at that stage, he would shut himself away from all outside interference and paint.

Once the paintings began to gain recognition, he stopped producing ceramics except for his own pleasure, and some miniatures he made in the late seventies.

His watercolors of this period, and the early fifties, were worked in the "wet-on-wet" style, in contrast to the technique he adopted later which is dependent upon his pen and ink drawing for their meaning. For the past twenty years his watercolors have been outlined in ink and filled in with color. Usually produced between midnight and 5:00 a.m., they are labeled "Midnight Sketch", with the hour and date by his signature. His book, *Christmas Fantasies,* published in 1977 is illustrated with these charming colored sketches.

Gaining recognition for his paintings was a struggle for De Grazia in his early career. He was helped immeasurably by the support of Raymond Carlson, then editor of "Arizona Highways", and the man who developed the magazine from little more than a Highway Department house organ to a respected internationally-known publication.

One of De Grazia's first exhibitions was in 1941 at the old Adams Hotel in downtown Phoenix. He has often said he thinks only two people saw the show. Fortunately, one of them was Carlson. Beginning that year, Carlson started using De Grazia's work in "Arizona Highways". Succeeding editors continued the practice and De Grazia's oils and watercolors, and his writing, became leading attractions in the magazine.

It was in the Summer of 1949 when my wife Leobarda and I visited his Tucson studio, that we first met Ted De Grazia, although we had been hearing about him from our artist friends since we first came to Arizona in 1942. Our interest had been whetted by the article about him in the March 1949 issue of "Arizona Highways" in which many of his paintings had been reproduced in color. There was also information about the ceramics he was doing, and which we had seen in the homes of friends. We wanted to include some of the ceramics in our recently opened gallery in Scottsdale. In addition to the ceramics, we also got some of the very few prints that he had made up to that time. It wasn't long before our customers were asking about original paintings after seeing the prints, with the result that we scheduled and held a one-man show of his paintings on February 5, 1950. Though advertised as a watercolor exhibit, we had about fifty paintings including both watercolors and oils. The show was a tremendous success, and became the foundation of our close friendship and a lasting business rapport. Over the three decades since, our gallery has continued to handle his original works of art.

"The Poor", Watercolor,
20" x 16", 1950

156

"Mexican Flowersellers",

The 1950's were a particularly productive time for De Grazia. He began sculpting, modeling first in clay and then casting his pieces in bronze. He has since created sculpture from many materials including ceramic, pewter, composition metals, wood and even one piece in iron which he cut and welded.

During this time he also made several striking pieces of jewelry in gold and silver, and over the years he has designed pieces which were made by other artisans. In 1952 he had a commission to design fabrics for a large firm in New York City.

Pewter Miniature Figurines,
Courtesy: Mr. Richard Smith,
Century Distributors Inc.
Tempe, Arizona

De Grazia created his first stone lithographs in 1949, but they were never marketed because the editions were so small. Between 1951 and 1959 he made several limited edition prints using his own version of the serigraphic, or silk screen, process. De Grazia screened a small part of the picture and hand painted the rest. These prints, then, are rightfully classified as "multiple originals", and have been popular substitutes for people who admire his work but cannot afford his original paintings.

De Grazia continued his exploration of print mediums in 1971 and 1972, creating a limited number of black and white etchings in those years. It was not until 1977, however, that he struck another stone lithograph, this one in color. Since then he has produced a number of colored lithographs and a few colored etchings. He has kept the editions of these prints relatively small which has made them collector's items.

"Packhorse II",
Stone-Lithograph, Dec. 1980,
22" x 30"

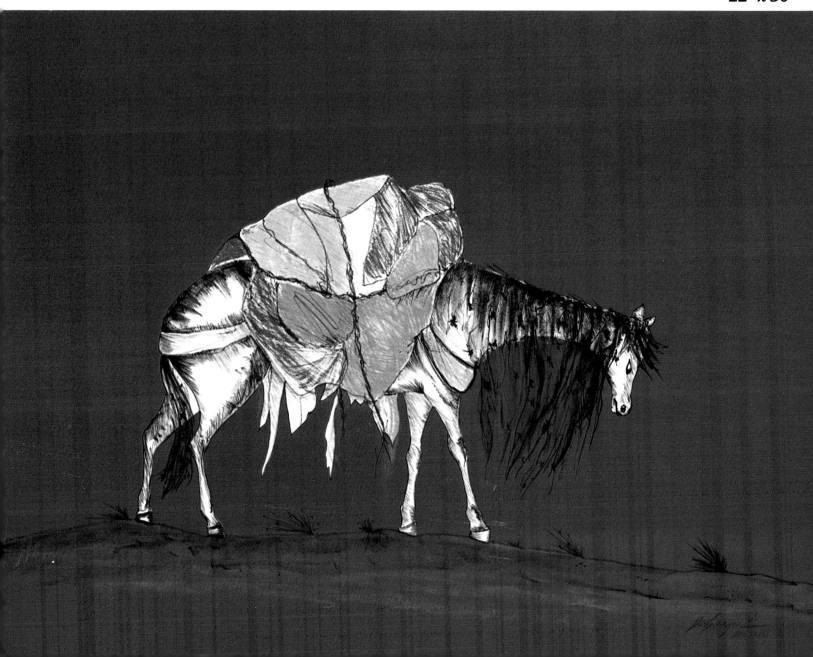

"Little Indian with Olla",
Stone-Lithograph, 30" x 22",
July 1980

162

De Grazia's ink drawings, usually quick studies for larger works, are a lesson in how his control of line and mark can speak of movement, serenity or convey a variety of emotions even without the pigment he uses so boldly in his paintings. In much the same way as the picture writing of the Indians he respects so deeply, De Grazia's pen makes itself clearly understood.

The artist draws in two different styles. One, a free-flowing technique with long lines made by continuous movement of his pen, is reserved for bullfight scenes and for the fantasy works drawn from his imagination. This style usually employs lighter lines than the dark, more precise drawings with which he offers information about historical figures or real-life Indian subjects. His sketches are strong in their black and whiteness, without tonal areas.

De Grazia and this powerful collection were accorded exceptional recognition in 1977. The Arizona House of Representatives devoted an entire morning session in May to eulogizing De Grazia for his artistic contributions to the state and to the "Arizona Highways Magazine", and the paintings were exhibited in the House foyer for some six months following. De Grazia's print, "Superstition Mountain," is to this day a gift House members reserve for important guests. Beautifully presented in a folder embossed with the Arizona seal, the print is accompanied by histories of the mountain and the state, and a biographical sketch of De Grazia.

Another recurrent theme in De Grazia's work is the bullfight. His book, *ah ha Toro,* published in 1967 captures the riveting drama of the clash of man and beast and reveals De Grazia's empathy for the customs and flavor of Mexico. His painting, "Classical Natural", is charged with motion and suspense as the matador, resplendent in his suit of light, taunts the raging bull.

In 1971 De Grazia published his book, *"De Grazia Paints The Signs of the Zodiac".* In this book are reproduced the twelve paintings that are his imaginative version of the signs of the Zodiac. These paintings have been reproduced as prints, as cards, on pewter jewelry and on jewelry wrought in other materials.

His own sign, Gemini, features two gun-laden soldiers marching in the army of Pancho Villa, one of his heroes. His Sagittarius, no centaur with bow and arrow, but an Indian brave astride a heavenly steed on a background of pinks and purples from a desert sunset, is a choice painting in this collection.

"Left-Handed Natural", Oil,

"Matador Taunts the Bull",

"Banderillero", Oil, 1966

"Picing", Oil,
24" x 18", 1966

167

The Bronzes:

In the 1960s De Grazia did a number of bronzes. His subjects, as always in all of his work, have been the Indian and religious figures that have figured so prominently in his paintings and books. One life size bronze of the "Yaqui Deer Dancer" is in the center of the courtyard of his "Gallery in the Sun". Smaller bronzes, done usually in small editions, have been of roadrunners, deer dancers, crown dancers, padres, carousel horses, wounded coyotes and Indians and padres on horseback. In the past two or three years he has once again turned to bronzes, and is still producing them.

"Ho'Ok", Cast Bronze

"Venus", Cast Bronze

"Apache Hunter",
Cast Bronze, 8"

"End of a Long Day",
Cast Bronze

172

"Drunken Mouse",
Cast Bronze

"Father Kino",
Cast Bronze, 7½"

173

"Little Prayer", Cast Bronze

"Angel", Cast Bronze

"Roadrunner", Cast Bronze

"Alone", Cast Bronze, 1981

"Woodcarrier", Bronze

175

ENAMELS are Precise, mechanical and scientific. TO ENAMEL is to fuse glass onto silver, copper or gold and other metels too at a temperature of 1350°F to/600°F FOR A MINUTE or LESS

Being a GEMINI I AM NOT consistant. thus I CAPITALIZE ON ARTISTIC IMPERFECTION thus NO TWO are ~~alike~~ — its FUN

176

The Enamels:

In his quest for new media in which to duplicate his art work De Grazia has experimented with many materials. In 1972 he did a series of pictures in enamel on copper. Each subject was done in an edition of either five, ten or fifteen. As in his earlier serigraphs no two copies of the same subject were ever the same, as he would change color and even shapes in doing the duplications, with the result that these enamels would best be described as "multiple-originals". The thirteen subjects of these enamels are shown in a paperback book by De Grazia, titled *"De Grazia Creates Enamels"*, published in 1975.

"Mother and Child", Enamel

"4 Horses in White", Enamel

"Pueblo Indian", Enamel

180

"Indians on Wagon", Enamel

"Bell Mare", Enamel

De grazia arizona el 1972

"Navajo and 2 Indians",
Enamel

"Mouse and Umbrella",
Enamel

"Indian Pueblo", Enamel

Products After De Grazia Motifs:

Needlepoint & Stained Glass

In recent years a number of craftsmen have asked for and received permission from De Grazia to use motifs from his paintings in the production of their particular products.

Among those that have proven most popular are the needlepoint designs produced by *Sundance Designs* in Tucson, Arizona, and the stained glass pieces produced by *Scottsdale Stained Glass* in Scottsdale, Arizona.

189

190

Stained Glass

Books by
De Grazia

In the 1950's De Grazia started to produce books on various subjects close to his heart. Prolific as in all other endeavors, the author De Grazia has since published a large number of volumes, some of them now out of print.

De Grazia's writing is terse and without artifice. Often strangely moving, as when he describes the sufferings and triumphs of the early colonizers such as Father Kino of Junipero Serra, but lucid and illuminating when he turns his pen to the myths and legends of his many Indian friends.

Some excerpts from the book "THE SUPERSTITION MOUNTAINS" appear in Part Two of this book and are a good example of De Grazia's writings.

BIBLIOGRAPHY:

De Grazia Silk Screen Earliest Books:

Mission in the Santa Catalinas, Book III,	1951
Papago and Yaqui Indians, Book 1,	1952
The Flute Player, Book II,	1952
Padre Nuestro, Book IV,	1953
The Blue Lady, Book V,	1957

De Grazia Books:

Kino (Booklet)	1966
Ah Ha Toro	1967
The Rose and the Robe	1968
Yaqui Easter	1968
Father Junipero Serra	1969
The Seri Indians	1970
Biographical Sketch	1971
M Collection	1971
Zodiac	1971
Superstition Mountains	1972
Cabeza De Vaca	1973
Moods	1974
Papago Legends	1975
Apache Indians	1976
Christmas Fantasies	1977
Padre Kino	1979
Graphics	1980

"Kateri Tekakwitha — Lily of the Mohawks", Bronze, 3 Feet Tall, 1979

196

De Grazia's production of art was radically changed in 1976. On May 12 of that year, he burned more than one hundred and fifty of his paintings in protest against tax statutes unfavorable to artists and their heirs. For three years following that extraordinary event, he painted no oils. Although he did begin to work in the medium again in 1979, he has produced very few oil paintings. His work now consists largely of pen and ink, watercolors, stone lithographs, etchings and some bronze sculpture.

Any artist's choice of materials and modes of expression are dependent on a multitude of variables in his moods, his life and his surroundings. De Grazia, having achieved success in almost every available means of artistic expression for nearly fifty years, is no different. Whatever medium he may use in the future, it is reasonable to assume that he will continue to work as long as he breathes in his own complex but honest fashion.

Through poverty and rejection he has always remained true to some inner need for creating a visionary world for himself and his people. And over the span of time that vast body of work has proved its steadfast universal appeal.

The End

INDEX:

DESIGN AND LAYOUT BY HARRY REDL
COMPOSED IN KORINNA
PRINTED BY IRONWOOD LITHOGRAPHERS
SCOTTSDALE, ARIZONA
ON MATTE FINISH KARMA TEXT
BOUND BY ROSWELL BOOKBINDING
PHOENIX

ISBN 0·940402·00·9

CHRYSALIS PUBLISHING, LTD